BLAIRSVILLE SENIOR HIGH SCHOOL
BLAIRSVILLE, PENNA.

Michael Vick

Jill C. Wheeler
AR B.L.: 4.7 Alt.: 743
Points: 0.5   MG

AWESOME ATHLETES

MICHAEL VICK

Jill C. Wheeler

ABDO Publishing Company

T 32433

L

visit us at
www.abdopublishing.com

Published by ABDO Publishing Company, 4940 Viking Drive, Edina, Minnesota 55435.
Copyright © 2007 by Abdo Consulting Group, Inc. International copyrights reserved in all
countries. No part of this book may be reproduced in any form without written permission from
the publisher. The Checkerboard Library™ is a trademark and logo of ABDO Publishing
Company.

Printed in the United States.

Cover Photo: Lee/WireImage.com
Interior Photos: AP/Wide World pp. 12, 15, 19, 24; Bob Rosato/Sports Illustrated p. 20;
    Corbis pp. 5, 8, 11, 14, 15; Getty Images pp. 7, 9, 13, 18, 21, 23, 26;
    Greg Foster/Sports Illustrated p. 27; John Iacono/Sports Illustrated p. 25;
    Peter Read Miller/Sports Illustrated p. 17; Wire Image pp. 6, 28-29

Series Coordinator: Rochelle Baltzer
Editors: Rochelle Baltzer, Megan M. Gunderson
Art Direction: Neil Klinepier

Library of Congress Cataloging-in-Publication Data

Wheeler, Jill C., 1964-
  Michael Vick / Jill C. Wheeler.
      p. cm. -- (Awesome athletes)
  Includes index.
  ISBN-10 1-59928-308-5
  ISBN-13 978-1-59928-308-1
  1. Vick, Michael, 1980---Juvenile literature. 2. Football players--United States--Biography--
Juvenile literature. I. Title. II. Series.

  GV939.V53W48 2006
  796.332092--dc22
                                                                              2005037939

Contents

Michael Vick

Michael Vick has been called the most electrifying player in the **National Football League (NFL)**. He is a talented athlete with blazing speed and a powerful arm. Since 2001, he has put those talents to work as a quarterback for the Atlanta Falcons.

Vick plays differently than most quarterbacks. He does not rely solely on passing the ball to other players. He is equally comfortable running it himself. In this way, some people have compared him to football great Steve Young.

Many people admire Vick. Yet some criticize the way he plays. They say he is inconsistent and does not meet the standards for a quarterback. In the 2004–2005 season, Vick **fumbled** the most in the NFL. He also had the worst rate for **sacks** in the league.

However, Vick posted a career-high running record that season. He ran for 902 yards (825 m). That was the third-highest total number of yards run by any NFL quarterback in history! This led some people to say Vick might make a better running back than quarterback.

Opposite Page: Despite criticism, Vick continues to prove himself a star player. Throughout his football career, he has set new records for NFL quarterbacks.

Vick's teammates disagree with the criticism. They also say Vick is among the most unselfish players because he doesn't care about his own numbers. Vick agrees that his main concern is bringing his team to victory. "I just do what it takes to win," he says.

Growing Up

Michael Dwayne Vick was born on June 26, 1980, in Newport News, Virginia. He has an older sister named Christina. He also has a younger brother, Marcus, and a younger sister, Courtney.

Michael was born to young parents. His mother, Brenda, worked at a store. His father, Michael, served in the military for two and a half years. So, he was unable to spend much time with the family.

Eventually, Michael joined the family in Newport News. However, he worked long hours in the local shipyards. He still found time to spend with young Michael. During that time, he taught his son what he knew about football.

Today, Michael (left) is not the only football star in his family. His brother Marcus (right) played for the Virginia Tech Hokies. And, his cousin Aaron Brooks is a quarterback for the Oakland Raiders.

Michael's father had been a skilled football player at one time. In fact, his nickname had once been "Bullet" because of his speed. When Michael was just three years old, his father taught him the basics of the game.

After Michael's announcement to join the 2001 NFL draft, his father *(left)* celebrated with him.

Discovering Sports

Michael grew up in the Ridley Circle housing project. At that time, drugs and gangs were common in the area. Michael watched his peers get involved with these things. But he knew he did not want that kind of future.

To stay away from trouble, Michael often went fishing in the nearby James River. Even if the fish weren't biting, sometimes he would cast a line just to escape.

In addition to fishing, Michael found he enjoyed sports. So, his mother encouraged him to play after-school sports. She figured this would help keep him out of trouble.

Michael played several sports, including baseball and basketball. However, football quickly became his favorite. Young Michael dreamed of being the next Steve Young or Randall Cunningham. These **NFL** quarterbacks were his heroes.

Steve Young was a quarterback for the San Francisco 49ers from 1987 to 1999. He became known for his outstanding passes. And, he was twice named the NFL's Most Valuable Player (MVP).

Growing up, Michael enjoyed many sports. But he became devoted to football and played whenever he could. He wanted to play in the NFL one day.

Freshman Starter

In 1994, Michael entered Warwick High School. Following the advice of his older cousin Aaron Brooks, Michael tried out for the school's football team. Coach Tommy Reamon had previously coached Brooks at Warwick. And, Reamon was a former player for the Kansas City Chiefs.

Michael made the Warwick Raiders's junior **varsity** football team his freshman year. As a quarterback, he threw an amazing 20 touchdown passes in his first six games!

Reamon quickly realized Michael was no ordinary quarterback. So midseason, Reamon made some changes to his teams. He moved the varsity quarterback to wide receiver. Then, Reamon made Michael the starting quarterback on the varsity team.

In his second game as starter, Michael threw for 433 yards (396 m) on just 13 **completions**. Reamon saw that Michael had much potential. So, he placed Michael in football camps during the off-season. And, he worked one-on-one with him.

By the end of his time at Warwick, Michael had turned in an amazing performance. As a senior, he was ranked among the nation's top five high school quarterbacks.

Clearly, Michael had the talent to earn a football **scholarship**. Many colleges contacted him. He seriously considered both Syracuse University in New York and Virginia Tech. He eventually chose Virginia Tech because it was closer to home.

Michael's exceptional throwing ability gained him a highly desired position on the Warwick Raiders football team. This was the start of much success on the field.

Virginia Tech

Michael began classes at Virginia Tech in fall 1998. However, he did not play in any football games for the Hokies that season.

Michael gets ready to pass

Coach Frank Beamer **redshirted** Michael. So, Michael practiced with the team, watched game videos, learned to read the defense, and observed the starting quarterback. This gave Michael time to develop his football skills at the college level before playing in games.

Off the field, Michael sometimes missed home. He often called his family. However, his initial homesickness didn't interfere with his field performance.

By spring, Michael's hard work during practices had impressed his coaches. The Virginia Tech coaches knew they had a likely winner. Michael set two records for Hokies quarterbacks. He could run 40 yards (37 m) in 4.33 seconds. And, he was able to leap 40.5 inches (102.9 cm)! He also had the ability to make up winning plays on the spot.

In fall 1999, Michael won the starting quarterback position for the Hokies. His first game was against the James Madison University Dukes. It ended in a 47–0 victory for the Hokies! Michael concluded the game with a somersault dive into the end zone for a touchdown. Nationwide, sports stations featured that play.

In his early years at Virginia Tech, Michael proved that he belonged on the field.

THE MAKING OF AN AWESOME ATHLETE

Michael Vick is one of the NFL's star athletes. He brings incredible speed and a forceful throw to the game.

1980	1994	1998	1999
Born on June 26 in Newport News, Virginia	Becomes starting quarterback for Warwick Raiders as a freshman	Begins classes at Virginia Tech	Finishes third in voting for the Heisman Trophy

How Awesome Is He?

Vick brings never-before-seen athletic abilities to the NFL. In 2004, he set a record for NFL quarterbacks during play-offs. He rushed the ball 119 yards (109 m)! Vick is also a talented passer. Among NFC players in the 2005 regular season, he was ranked eighth in passes resulting in a touchdown.

Player/Ranking	Touchdown Passes
Matt Hasselbeck/#1	24
Drew Bledsoe/#4	23
Michael Vick/#8	**15**
Brad Johnson/#12	12

MICHAEL VICK

TEAM: ATLANTA FALCONS
NUMBER: 7
POSITION: QUARTERBACK
HEIGHT: 6 FEET
WEIGHT: 215 POUNDS

2000	**2001**	**2003**	**2004**
Plays in the Sugar Bowl	Becomes the number one NFL draft pick and signs with Atlanta Falcons	Plays in the Pro Bowl for the first time	Leads Falcons to second play-off appearance in his second full season starting

- Finished behind Ron Dayne (first) and Joe Hamilton (second) in the 1999 Heisman Trophy voting
- Signed a deal in 2004 worth an estimated $130 million that made him the NFL's highest-paid player
- Became first African-American quarterback taken as the number one draft choice

Highlights

Almost Champions

The James Madison game was the start of an unbelievable season for the Hokies. The team had finished the previous season at 8–3. But with Michael as starting quarterback, they ended 1999 at 11–0.

The Florida State Seminoles also finished the 1999 season undefeated. On January 4, 2000, the Seminoles and the Hokies met in the Sugar Bowl. Early in the game, the Seminoles made three touchdowns. However, Michael helped the Hokies battle to a razor-thin 29–28 lead.

Virginia Tech ended up losing the game 29–46. Yet Michael came out a hero. Football fans nationwide noticed his one-of-a-kind playing style. For Michael, the Sugar Bowl was a fitting end to an amazing season.

The 1999 season had been a record-breaking time for Michael. He set a record among college athletes nationwide for effective passing by a freshman. And, he was named the Big East Offensive Player of the Year.

Michael turned in an incredible performance at the Sugar Bowl. He completed 15 of 29 passes, for a total of 225 running yards (206 m).

Michael also finished third in voting for the Heisman Trophy. This is the most highly regarded award in college football. Each year, it is given to the top-performing U.S. college football player.

As a quarterback, it is Michael's responsibility to call plays for his team.

Michael's second season playing for the Hokies proved much tougher. It began bright, with a 6–0 start. But then Michael sprained his ankle. As a result, he missed an important game against the University of Miami Hurricanes. The Hokies lost that game and their chance for another undefeated season.

Yet, Michael came back to lead the Hokies in the 2001 Gator Bowl. The Hokies beat the Clemson University Tigers 41–20. This was the first Gator Bowl the Hokies had ever won! Michael was named his team's Most Valuable Player (MVP).

Michael's amazing spins and reverses have earned him the nickname Houdini after the famous magician and escape artist.

NFL Bound

Michael's top performance with the Hokies had gained him widespread attention among **NFL scouts**. Chances were good he could be the number one **draft** pick. So in January 2001, Michael announced that he was quitting college to join the NFL draft.

This was just the news the Atlanta Falcons were waiting to hear. They traded other players to make sure they could get Michael. And on May 9, 2001, Michael signed a six-year contract with the team. It was worth nearly $62 million!

NFL scouts watch Michael and other possible draft picks during a workout

At that time, Dan Reeves was the head coach for the Falcons. Like Michael's past coaches, Reeves decided to take things slow for Michael's first season. Chris Chandler remained the starting quarterback. Reeves only let Michael play in certain situations.

But in fall 2001, Michael began to see more field time. Chandler suffered injuries. So, Reeves often put Michael on the field. Michael even got to start two games.

Michael's first professional game was against the Pittsburgh Steelers on August 3, 2001. He completed five out of seven passes during the game!

Sometimes, Michael played like an **NFL** star. Other times, he made mistakes. He often turned the ball over to the other team.

Part of Michael's problem quickly became clear. The Falcons's offensive plays were hard to memorize. Sometimes, Michael focused too much on remembering the play names instead of playing the game. So, he spent the off-season studying the playbook and watching game videos. He wanted a fresh start for the next season.

NFL Success

Vick's hard work paid off. At the start of the 2002–2003 season, the Falcons's coaches released Chandler and made Vick their starting quarterback. They also simplified their playbook.

It was clear that Vick was comfortable in his new role. The Falcons had ended the 2001–2002 season with a record of 6–10. But with Vick as starter, their 2002–2003 season was brighter. At one point, Vick led his team to seven wins in a row! People began talking about him as a new kind of quarterback.

The Falcons piled up wins all the way to the **play-offs**. The ended their regular season with a record of 9–7. Then, they faced the Green Bay Packers on chilly Lambeau Field for the National Football Conference (NFC) wild-card game.

The Packers had never lost a play-off game at home. However, Vick and his team beat the odds. The Falcons won in a 27–7 blowout! This was Vick's first play-off win. He also landed his first spot in a Pro Bowl. Only the best **NFL** players get to compete in these all-star games.

The Falcons competed in the
NFC play-offs as a wild-card
team. This means that although
they did not win their division,
they qualified for the play-offs
as a runner-up. In each
conference, two teams earn
wild-card spots in the play-offs.

Unfortunately, Vick's 2003–2004 season ended before it even began. On August 16, he broke his leg during training camp. The injury kept him out of the first 11 games. Without Vick, the Falcons's record slid to 2–9. But when Vick returned, he helped

Even after a hard practice, Vick does not tire of signing autographs.

steer the team to a few wins. The Falcons ended the season at 5–11.

The Falcons enjoyed more success in the 2004–2005 season. With Vick back in the game, they became division champions. This put them face-to-face with the Philadelphia Eagles for the NFC championship game. Yet not even Vick's talents could stop the Eagles. The Eagles beat the Falcons 27–10 on their way to the **Super Bowl**.

Vick leaps upside down during a game against the New York Giants

Vick Today

Today, Vick continues to impress on the field. Off the field, his hobbies include fishing, golfing, and playing video games. He also enjoys spending time with his family.

Vick believes it is important to recognize young football fans. This is partly because of an encounter from his own childhood.

When Vick was ten years old, he attended a college football game. Outside the stadium, he spotted Bruce Smith of the Buffalo Bills. Vick excitedly yelled, "Bruce!" Smith replied, "What's up?" and gave him the peace sign. After this exchange, Vick vowed to reach out to kids if he ever became a football star himself.

Today, Vick has followed through on his promise. For the past three years, he has volunteered at an Atlanta, Georgia, homeless shelter. During the holiday season, he hands out gifts to children.

Vick receives a grand introduction before a game

Vick reaches out to children in other ways, too. In 2004, he opened the Michael Vick Camp. There, children ages 8 to 16 can play football with Vick and learn more about the game. "Getting to be out here with these kids reminds me of why I play football," Vick said. "It's about team building, friendship, leadership, and learning how to win."

Vick enjoys sharing his talent with children. Some of the best high school, college, and NFL coaches and players are instructors at his camp. They teach the campers about basic football skills and team competition.

Glossary

completion - a forward pass in football that is caught by a receiver.

draft - an event during which sports teams choose amateur players.

fumble - to lose hold of a football while handling it or running with it.

National Football League (NFL) - a professional football organization in the United States consisting of the National Football Conference (NFC) and the American Football Conference (AFC). Each conference has 16 teams.

play-off - a series of games played after the end of a regular sports season to determine which teams will compete in a championship.

redshirt - to keep a college athlete from participating in sport competition for an entire school year.

sack - to tackle a quarterback behind the line of scrimmage. This is the imaginary line across the field where a football is placed at the beginning of a play.

scholarship - a gift of money to help a student pay for instruction.

scout - someone sent to discover new talent, such as athletes or entertainers.

Super Bowl - the NFL championship game played annually by the winners of the American and National football conferences.

varsity - the main team that represents a school in athletic or other competition. A junior varisty team has members not qualified for the varsity team.

Web Sites

To learn more about Michael Vick, visit ABDO Publishing Company on the World Wide Web at **www.abdopublishing.com**. Web sites about Vick are featured on our Book Links page. These links are routinely monitored and updated to provide the most current information available.

Index